BEAST

Praise for Beast

"*There is plenty of Circe, and plenty of Caliban, too, in the poems of Frances Justine Post's book* Beast. *Carl Jung would have nodded in affirmation at the way in which myth and archetype pulse and flow under the surface of her poems—wolf, whale, cannibal, fire, doll. Her monologues cast the speaker's self into these tableaux, and it's hard to convey the detailed viscerality with which Post renders the human psyche—in all its needy, vengeful, rueful, generous and knowing configurations. 'What have you been killing, my dear? / Let me wipe your chin.' Post's theme is hopeless love, but there is so much bravado, courage, insight, and self-knowledge in the poems that* Beast *feels like a weird, wild, somewhat frightening party. Not to mention the sensuous, acrobatic flamboyance of Post's remarkable writing, which carries this psychic carnival all proudly into Art.*"

—*Tony Hoagland, author of* What Narcissism Means to Me

"*Frances Justine Post's* Beast *is an intimate and startling exploration of a many-faceted, unmoored self. Here, the speaker prepares for disaster in the shadow of a volcano; crawls deep inside an enormous whale, lying down 'on the bed of its liver'; finds herself transformed into a pack of hounds or, later, into a cannibal consuming the body of the beloved whose loss colors these poems. With ventriloquistic energy, musical innovation, and fascinating intelligence, Post examines the shifting psyche's relationship with a world of natural beauty, grief, joy, and chaos. This is a terrific debut collection of poems.*"

—*Kevin Prufer, author of* In a Beautiful Country

BEAST

poems by Frances Justine Post

Augury Books
New York, New York

Published in the United States of America
First Edition

Cover Images by Cecelia Post
Front: *You Made Me (Sewing)*
Back: *Flood*
Book Design by Daniel Estrella
ISBN: 978-0-9887355-2-1

For reproduction inquiries or other information,
please visit www.augurybooks.com.

Acknowledgements

Many thanks to the editors of the journals in which these poems first appeared, sometimes in earlier versions: *American Letters & Commentary, Boston Review, Denver Quarterly, DIAGRAM, JERRY, The Kenyon Review Online, La Petite Zine, Love Among the Ruins, The Massachusetts Review, Pleiades, Quarterly West, Verse Daily,* and *Western Humanities Review.* Also, thank you to the editors of *DIAGRAM III: The Best of DIAGRAM Anthology* and the Wave Books Tumblr for featuring my poems.

I would like to thank my family for their support, inspiration, and unwavering encouragement. Ma and Pa, without your guidance and support, your eccentricities and humors, I wouldn't see the world the way I do. Lia, you and your art challenge, inspire, and motivate me every day.

Special thanks to the professors and friends whose insight, intelligence, and support helped shape these poems into better versions of themselves: Mary Jo Bang, Whit Bones, Lucie Brock-Broido, Jocelyn Casey-Whiteman, Timothy Donnelly, Deborah Gorlin, Tony Hoagland, Richard Howard, Paul Jenkins, Jameelah Lang, Elizabeth Lyons, Krista Manrique, Karyna McGlynn, Kevin Prufer, Camille Rankine, Elizabeth Whittlesey, and Annabelle Yesseul Yoo.

Thank you to the organizations and universities who offered time, space, and/or support in the writing of these poems: Columbia University, Inprint, the Lower Manhattan Cultural Council, *Poets & Writers,* the University of Houston, and the Unterberg Poetry Center at 92nd Street Y.

All my thanks and gratitude to Kate Angus and Kimberly Steele, the amazing editors of Augury Books.

Contents

IV.

V.

for my family

Self-Portrait as Beast

I put on my face. This one is wolfish,
        covered in whorls of black and gray fur.
My whiskers flex and fall; I comb them

        with my nails. My teeth are broken in places.
                Depending on the light, I am glossy
or made of shadows. When I walk, my skin,

loose, follows with a slight delay. What did I wear
        when we were new? Must have been the curly
one, lambish. Later, I was the blind ostrich,

        my face a sad block, all eye and beak, hiding
                in the sand. I chew my paws and pace
the bedroom. My fur is furrowed and sweaty.

I pant. I pant and growl softly, bare my teeth
        at you on your way out. I heard everything,
do you believe it? The uneasy feeling

        of a stranger by your side. Turn around;
                I am the stranger. Go on, run away now,
run away on your dainty little hooves.

I.

Marionette

You find my heart—four tough little mouths
inhaling, exhaling with a liquid
                mechanical flap—
        and push your finger against the current.

The blood sings to itself, humming from blue
to red, washing through its orderly
                highways, each suspended
        in a controlled tangle from my clean, white

architecture. Before sleep, the pulse in my ear
sounds like someone walking
                down an empty corridor,
        but mostly it's a twitch, a murmur

under the skin. Press down my lungs and they empty
like bellows, outing a rudimentary
                language. Let go,
        and I gasp as if swallowing

the whole world. I wanted to swallow it,
so I wrote it. And I wrote you here,
                in front of the window
        out of which the leaves are turning red

and then losing it. How my body loved you,
you touched me and the blood
                rushed to the spot
        to warm your fingertips.

Self-Portrait in Maelstrom

Knocking at the window, a splash interrupts us,
your tongue in my ear. The water rises

      like clasping, a familiar bite of salt.
    Now part of the eddying, we are swept

with the tide to the living room.
There's the writing desk walking forward

      surrounded by its cloud of ink; grandmother
    unearthed in her silks. Sometimes my leg

will go a little dead when we are breathless.
We are pulled up the whirlpool of the spiral

      staircase, through the French doors a stingray
    has smashed like a bird that sees only open sky

in the glass. The rooms make sense now as caves;
the roof has lifted. What will we see

      when morning comes? A second birth?
    Forests of kelp? A hook on a dangling wire?

A gull preening on a sargasso raft,
that wicked bird always laughing? A boat

      pushes towards us. It's a trap. Do you feel
    like trapping or do you just want to live

on the salt? The sail rent, the paint
a dirty pool. The clouds, red when we met.

Twinspeak

Hold our feet, our four that are not fingers.
We so like to be petted. We've been missing

you. We sick, gray, would like a distillation
of all experience we might miss so better

to make the decision. What we're after is
I want a boat-ride. I want Alaska. Everywhere

is full of greenery; the difference is the sea
level, but how are we to divide? We saw

the hawk perched on the thrush—still flying
however pinioned—and did nothing.

This means that we identified. So who
the hawk and who the thrush? No one wants

to be the hawk but otherwise the equation
wouldn't work. Won't you join us? With you

coming around, the stars must necessarily scratch
the sky, meaning we are still, the rest keeps moving.

We'll take the blue from your eyes and give it away
so we are more alike. Hold us first in your way,

with warmth and a certain ambivalence. We'll quiet
then we'll not. We'll speak in the singular.

Self-Portrait as a Pack of Hounds

We move as one, a sea of eyes, yellow,
        unnatural, our ears dangling down, our paws
slipping on the dried leaves. We're made to want you.

        Your face in a snarl, your red coat, your black-shod
           feet tucked up to clear a ditch.
Why did you leave us here? We don't know where this is.

We slobber and peal down the trail. Our noses searching
        for your pulse. Nuzzle, growl, we dig
and fight and dig, crashing through the brambles.

        Your scent a fever. Some fluff from your tail,
           red-tipped gray. Our love a frenzy.
What will we do when we have you?

Abandon

Last night I dreamed my legs stopped working. I was
          your doll. You dragged me everywhere, first by hand,
              then by hair. Later you dropped me off a cliff,
which is when I woke. You've migrated to my side.

The trouble with this night is it's come before anything else.
          I won't say it, but I'm asking *will there be more?*
              More silky, more abandon, more cheek
to cheek, more tumbling, more pivot and pressing?

And, furthermore, who are you? Don't wake,
          I won't ask. Out the window, it sounds like rain.
              The all-weather house sparrow perches
on rusting steps. She is warbling (listen) *stop it stop it stop it.*

Self-Portrait as Equestrian

At first you were a horse, then a man ready
        to be let out of your stable. I own you.
I won't let you. If only you could outrun

        your harness. You smell of sweat and leather.
            The sound of your tail twitching, snakelike.
You stamp your tip-toe feet; so small to hold aloft

your body. I wander in the sun, feeling ugly and humid
        under my jacket. You are responsible.
The ash on my hands looks like old blood.

        I burned up the field, but it's coming back,
            spiteful, its green shoots perfect for you.
I notice everywhere bruises the shape of teeth,

little spots bleeding their color out. Your pink mouth
        and your teeth all in a row. I want it to end
just so it can start all over. This is how we live:

        I say no. At night, you sleep right on top of me, heavy
            on my chest. In my sleep, I dream of sleep.
I sleep so well, your hair in my mouth. I can't speak.

Heart Hunted, Was Caught

Heart desirous, has four lives. Heart, a thief,
greedy above all things, tell-tale, your cheating

heart, ugly, green. Heart peers. Tastes of iron.
Like a grenade, pull. Hard. Heart speaks

with stutter, with limp, sweetheart, what murmur,
what pinch. What hope heart had, lost it. Poor heart,

bloody. Heart froze in your throat. Sick.
Heart sunk, has no more room. A cricket's cage,

a beehive. Unblock heart. I sat next to heart,
vacant, wordless, bone. Heart hooked

like a trout. Heart whispers *I am everywhere
under you.* Heart dropped, a piece of soap,

a hot potato. The teeth of your black, burnt-out
heart. A prairie with the sound of clapping.

Heart, empty, bays at the moon. Heart, a citizen
of gore, a pitcher of poppies. Changeable,

quaking, s*hhh shhh,* stubborn, wistful, shudders,
lets loose what it should be holding fast.

Self-Portrait in the Body of a Whale

We come upon the body of a whale, a fresh beaching.
      It smells like a thousand fishes.
I crawl in on the carpet of its tongue, seeking the injury out.

      Outside, you cough and look away as I squint
            through the eye at you. I dig into the room
its ribs make and squat in the warm gloom. The heart,

a chandelier, hangs down, ringed with veins. Here and there
      the skin, thinned by hermit crabs, lets in the light
like a stained glass window with blood red panes.

      I lie down on the bed of its liver as the tide fills the body,
          each wave, higher. You give the whale a kick
I almost didn't feel and gesture towards the dunes,

backing away, disappearing. Is this who you really are?
      This is where I live now like a barnacle,
stern and grumpy. If you try to move me, I will cut you.

II.

The Miners

Our field the color of kiwi   I stay down under the reeling stalks
the dirt rich with manure   smelling like blood   minerals
in front of my nose   a piece of broken corncob   stripped
like half a jaw   with teeth intact

I go to sleep with your unseeing sliver of eye on me   and dream
of breaking teeth   a mouthful of jagged white and marrow
on waking your tender snore   reverberates   it's nearly time

There are many steps   I don't know how   though I've counted
do you remember   nervy and lightheaded   I see a few low
morning stars   a grid of moons smearing   before it goes black

Clip clop   the wheels hit a groove   down we go
sweat and dirt on my nicely bleached T   night's not black
down here   but lime-white   bone mixed with dirt
and everything combustible   we paint ourselves into a corner
muck it up with our smudgy prints

Coal already smells like burning   what we were sent here for
we're left behind   muffled and snuffed   waiting for the wall
of water   or the like   rocks   mud   to seal us
as after a river dammed   at least we would be clean

Stained the color of it   oil slicked with a sheen
like we've been rubbed   too long on paper   the world
is cave   and life above us heavy   bearing down

Someone starts to hum   it's too hot for that   sing something
cold   a cold lullaby   lull us down   we've been down here
so long and lonely   each light blinking out

Empty am so empty   juiced and jangled here   like a fence
made of willow   we begin to grow   where hammered

Outside in your red rain slicker   a catch in your throat   waiting
for the rain to stop   me to come up finally freed   a bobbing log

III.

Beckett Wolf

A sudden revelation, a tinge
like a blush, and there quivered and felt

the world come closer, some pressure
of rapture, split. The smoke fades and assembles

itself round an emptiness about the heart
of life, untidy. Stargazing with the rooks

flaunting up, so before a battle begins
the horses paw the ground. It is with the heart

one loves; you are confusing it.
The green linoleum, a tap dripping;

it is strange, still. Watch at night the distant
city lights, the lightships and lighthouses,

the curlews, the clink like distant silver
of the hammers, the tomatoes, hyacinths,

pinks and seedlings, groves, grottoes,
artificial lakes with swans. All's over;

the sheet stretched and the bed narrow.
The sounds come thin and chill and you,

left blackberrying in the sun. But this question
of love; it comes back too often, but often.

Birds of North America

A cloud like a blimp lists eastward
until it hides behind a building where
        a man on his balcony watches me.
    I close the blinds and turn. You enter

with your specific sounds (keys, boots, paper;
drop, remove, place) and your coat clinging snow.
        I look at you with hunger
    and patience; you returning, knowing

what's coming next, which way we go, the directions,
but not telling. Lights dim; we retire to the dark.
        Out the window, faint music
    or voices or blizzard and always the shush

and bang of automotives and bicycles with chains.
Soon a garbage truck will arrive to root and trill
        at the corner. Wait. The logic doesn't work.
    If I discovered you, you couldn't have

discovered me. For too long I was dim
and clouded, observed myself with interest
        but no investment. You didn't flush me out,
    but that you were there with a net is indicative.

Like a bird who's hit a window finds her way
to a bush—it was the opposite. I came alive and moved
        outdoors, my low song producing,
    finally, an answerable diagnostic hum.

Self-Portrait as Witch

Unmoored, my body, stiff as a boat, drifts
      with the muddy current away.
On the banks, your muscles relax. They were coiled

      against me so long, I couldn't see it.
          You're growing small, blurred,
your colors mixing in with the woods.

The lights like soft discs turn this way and that,
      yellow, gold. You weave in place,
the water to your chest, your arms thrashing

      a kind of semaphore. Too late. I turn my head
          and half the world and half what's under,
half light, half murk and a mist of suspended grit.

My eyes follow the weed snaking down,
      the current waves them goodbye to me.
By dusk, I've cleared the village and swallows

      swallows! swallows! swallows! diving all around
          wings whirring, forked tails jerking.
Don't fly so high who's made only of feathers.

Pastoral

I

On the telephone you told me you were chasing
a horse through Francis Marion Forest. But you lied.

You dreamed you were chasing a horse through Francis
Marion Forest. I've come to understand all your lies

are like wishes. Freud says horses represent love
in dreams: I looked it up. From our recent conversations,

I imagine your pursuit was halfhearted. You chase
the horse away, holding a whip but also a carrot.

II

I dream I am in the body of a pig. This is not a lie.
Low and heavy, my expanse of skin extends

behind me glowingly. Freud says the pig represents
lack of spirituality and ambivalence about love.

There is a herd of us, maybe twenty. We appear
to be in an etching by someone like Bruegel.

We root for potatoes and other tubers. We lie
in the mud, half-submerged, or pull hay from the caged

bales. Our snouts stretch into aspects of happiness,
our soft ears falling forward to cover our eyes.

III

Now I'm lying, or wishing. Alone in the pen, I stick my head
through the low slats of the split-rail fence. All the others—

glossy brown or onyx or palomino, amber and snorting
with feeling—gallop and chase in the next field over.

Self-Portrait in the Shadow of a Volcano

It doesn't lurch exactly, not to the eye; it hums.
Little pills of dirt roll down the bank. It's not a rumbling

you hear, but a tearing. A few dogs dash, intent,
through town. A fox pair gambols through the park,

climbs a tree. Fog, or is it smoke, inches down, a smell
of eggs, a muddying. The vegetation will not singe

just yet. You knew this was possible. The sky
jaundiced, the ocean, slate; the waves with their

tops blown off. A beaching, a tightening,
a confusion of throat, a clench in your animal gut.

Last night you dreamed of birth, something you'd
forgotten. A sharp burn, a tenderness about the center,

then out came all the shades of red vermilion crimson
pale tendrils mammalian membrane strange clots a nail

a cord blue a tooth, but is it something that must be assembled?
Follow the signs, you were warned. It won't stop.

You can't wait for something that will never be told to you,
weatherman or no doctor. Natural won't change disaster.

Afterlife

All day my boots try to make me fall,
        but I hold up, put them in the corner,
                punished with dry rot. Come back
you broke me. Shut those birds up.

I open the window to let them fly out.
        Does this end where it started?
                Stop that banging radiator behind you.
To know you want no other is not enough.

You turned me off, so coldly. You wanted this.
        If this is the end, then take it all.
                Even the windbreak of cedars in Indiana
where I'm not from but from and must let go.

Self-Portrait in Whirlwind

At the door a sound, a heartbeat,
something elemental. The house begins to shake,

window panes to shiver, crack.
Out the window, past the bright yellow

wheat, a contrasting cloud touches
down or over the sound a spout slaps

and circles, plunges, water going up,
upends a boat, breaches all those tons.

Takes a hand, a shoe, incites terror,
a drowning. Inside, clipped wings,

the red fruit of the thorn tree. In climb,
in crawl a man going round, hard to kick

against the pricks of dirt, too late tonight
to be dragged out. The house dismantled

into air, whitewashed clapboards dispersed,
breath blown out. It's a ladder reaching

down or up, what will become of us.
A piece of land widowed, leaded, any sip

of air. What's left: dust on skin translucent.
What's wanted: what's absent, to fight

or fill, tendons, veins like letters, corners
to bruise, to sink teeth into. Next time shut

the screen to bedlam. Take it all but let me
down. This dream that will return of a looming

eye and angry toss, heavy cumulus curling
at the edges, an anvil over moving blue.

How to Build the Coral Reef

Break the bridge. Explode it down to the barge,
        a cloud of pigeon, smoke, dust, shards, nests,
                the bones of a builder so they say.
The barge must be new, no part rotted

or mildewed and a tug boat painted freshly red.
        Truck it out, the barge and bridge,
                all those miles to the Gulf Stream.
There will be dangers in the gloom,

those wild eyes that watch, barracuda,
        sea snakes and octopuses, slithering,
                clasping, shooting from dark corners.
Can you see through the murk

that which you knew all these years? It has been pulled
        out from under you. The creatures
                will arrive and live and die
and the coral will build, a craggy shelf,

elkhorn, brain. If it's brain, be careful,
        it will tattoo your leg. It's not your job
                to worry about the aftermath.
You just do the thing; that's how you live.

IV.

The Spectators

—there, before the spectators ringed round, the countless unmurmuring dead

It doesn't happen as it is supposed to.   You stop your dying
and go on living   you're waiting   don't want a funeral.

We stoop down and stay to the end   we follow your fevered
body into the cold   wind streaming through the screens.

We carry you on our backs   along the line of oleanders
to the marsh.   We become you in your dying.   Your hair coats

our necks.   We look sideways with your hooded eyes   for a path
to the water.   Like ducks we run along the surface   fall through.

We are old   you are new   our ears full of flutter
and vertigo.   We put you in a chair   roll you down the dunes.

We knew you when you were young.   We walk together
the palms fan and crash in this heat   we take you to the races

so you can smell the horses.   We hide behind the trees
re-emerge.   We are just shadows   flickering in the corner.

You will see us presently.   We like it when you talk to us
it brings back a certain feeling   of earth beneath our feet.

Black hill   black leaves blotted.   The crows   territorial
frighten off.   Trespassing this inert place   you've covered

your tracks.   We find a hair   a print   a rind   we lose
our breath   in the cold shock of stream.   Shapes shift

opaque shift   fallen shift.   We wake   in a cave of roots
as sidewinders   as creepers   a clinging weed.   Bewildered

forlorn   we ache   we hunger.   Night sweats.   We find
you up the river bed   our faces your reflection   split.

There is a tear in our fabric   it leaks a sound   a soft
whistling that reminds.   You sulk and gnash and turn away

what beautiful resistance.   We're there wherever you look
optical.   Take something of us with you   a nail   a tooth

our rope of hair   wrapped round your wrist   brittle.
We travel a dusky path   river to bridge   without stopping

our feet slow   breaking through.   The pines hover
crack   the sap sticky on our lips   when we pause to lick.

We try to find you hiding in these woods   the trees so tall
as to obliterate light.   We wait behind the waterfall

for your form to fall   a red flash.   We jostle and twitch
in the narrow cave   our fingers reaching through the mist

the rocks oozing.   Tell us which way you've gone.   We wake
on a pond waxed over with ice.   Our hands trapped   reaching

for warmth.   Around a flock of rooks huddles   a drift insulates.
We begin to feel a little life nibbling   at the moss we've grown.

Panting   we are still   hobbled.   A sharp hissing and hurtling
the pond shifts inwardly   there is a tapping down below.

A sound like a flight of distant crows   a lack of sound
a shushing.   Over us a dirty haze   muffles.   And again

that winging   too cold to speak.   Our feathers frozen
won't catch air.   We search leaf   brush.   Lichen   we grow

slowly   not to end.   Are chilled until we feel heat   a fire
you set.   Numb we begin to see   the sun silhouettes the trees.

Our jaws   sore from clench and cutting.   What bound us
ice and grasses   bitten through.   We screech and hoot down

the glacial hill   rolled over and under   silt and finger lakes.
Drift and watershed   the hills slide us to the shore where you ebb

away on a floe.   Still over-shoeing snow   we run and trudge
until your perch melts   blue and transparent like an inner lid

you come ashore.   The cold's receded   a kettle stream
a river warm.   Clear to muddy churning.   Evergreen to oak.

We return to your birthplace.   The corn at night is full
of watching.   We pass through cotton fields trailing black husks

tufts.   Spin them into a long thread to stitch around your waist
each of ours.   We are hemmed and humbled.   We flutter

and twine in the mud   you among us lean and sleek.
We vibrate   hum.   You take some sweet from the honeysuckle.

You seek a swamp   float in shade and sediment.   Cypress
we're all root.   Climb the tree   and dream of falling.

Gather the magnolia leaves   split the flesh from the veins.
Your mouth bruised with berries   pollen blondes your hair.

Before you go   feel where we were   the whirring too low
to hear.   You creak the floorboards   in the sleepless night.

Your hair loosed   water-lit.   The ocean black reflects no light.
We pull you down   the blanket up.   We tuck our skins

beneath your back.   The edges begin to bleed and blur   a fog
reaches from shore to shore.   We flicker   become more clear.

V.

Self-Portrait as the Crumbs You Dropped

We, the crows that eat the crumbs. The preening
        crows, glossy, we want you lost. We, the feather
falling to your shoulder. The dust in your pocket,

        the ink spot, black and brittle. We, the whiskers
            creeping up your neck. We sit on your cheek
and grow. We, the sweat on your back, spreading.

We, the gnats in your ear. The hand that slaps. The rock
        that trips. The nail, blue, that sloughs off. The blood,
dead. We, the bear that sniffs the nail. That follows you

        stiff-legged, massive. We, the drool. The pelt.
            In the looming dark. Our rich smell of earth.
Your perspiration betrays you. A twig snaps. Behind you.

Looking at the Photographs

In this one, you're overdeveloped,
          a gray clot on a chair. Your voice
                    in my ear, I can't make it out exactly,
but it means you're feeling something.

Here you thrash, a see-through ghost
          with statue feet. But I'm not feeling
                    anything, my strange, tell-tale body
won't release. Too late to matter, I've already

pulled my heart from its cushion.
          It hangs out front like a carnival flower
                    that when squeezed shoots you
in the face. *Look how the harbor lights*

reach and the boats look like flames
          at midnight. Tell me something good
                    will come of this. Now
to *Hawaii* or *the volcano* or *notice how the fire*

flickers in the oven or *the rain-soaked tent*
          or *dissecting table* or *the ocean*
                    as a bowl where the fish
bleakly push, all in one direction.

Self-Portrait in Antarctica

There's a door down a path I never noticed
        before, a brass hand holds the knocker.
Inside it's Antarctica. Apparently,

        Antarctica is just white and ice
           and the water when you're in it
cuts like a mirror might. Here is a white fox

who has my eyes, black, my lips, pursed.
        The only color in Antarctica
is a drop of blood falling from its red tongue.

        What have you been killing, my dear?
        Let me wipe your chin.
I am tired of difficult love; yours is the only

constant heart. It's time to close mine down,
        pack it up for safe keeping.
In the ice below your feet, it glows like emergency.

Hover, Coo

This dream of a bird, strange, tangled up. A hybrid:
a bunting and an owl with those sad wet eyes, clacking bill,

moony face, feathered with indigo, lichen, gray, lazuli
rainbow of oil as if dipped in, iridescent, painted like susans

and predatory, of song and coyness, perch, a flit, hover, bark, a *coo*
a cry, a warble, an undulating sigh. This bird tangled, netted,

is trapped against the screen clinging, panting, can fly
but without joy, can see, but through a cloud, a fog

of its own breathing. Carnivore, you want to put it in your mouth.
Just a slip of, a pocket of, an envelope of skin, feather, bone.

Hypnotize with smoothing the wild, the fussing and gnashing.
Its feet unperch and it sleeps, unblinking other, uncanny

when the unreal becomes real. Pluck the suffocation out.
Lay the bird down in a scattering of dun-colored leaves

which then become bird, like animation but more a dream brought
to life, the frightening of what is known and long familiar.

Self-Portrait as Murmuration

Now halo, now torpedo, now a black planet
        exploding, bright and smeared. Now stars in an inky
atmosphere. Now a disassembled man, a god

        like a sleepwalker. Now black water spreading, now black
                hills with white lakes, a funnel cloud, a rope.
Now shadow, now gutter, now something escaping

under a door, now water rocking in a bowl. Now DNA,
        the strands twisting, leading a path away from you.
Now to roost, now something cutting like freedom.

How to Build the Island

To begin, stiff grasses. Depending on the season,
        they must be brown, gray, or green, leaf or spring
                green only, no hints of blue; there may be yellow.
Then add the mud. For the marsh, pluff, and for the ocean,

sand. Make it fine so it can be hard or soft, depending
        on the tide, and make sure it can be winded to sting.
                Of course, water. Salt for the ocean
and brackish for the inlets. The former must not be clear.

When you add the fishes with their scales
        like sandpaper, you will not see them again
                until they want you to. By brushing your calf
with tentacles or fins, or causing ripples and dark shadows,

or appearing underfoot. Watch them from a distance, cresting
        or roiling the water, following a boat.
                The boats come later and are inferior contraptions.
Then, the trees that you will imitate in their finery.

The bushes that are feathered and berried and the flowers
        that always have company. You will be formed last
                and most crudely. *Who chose this face for me?*
You have no choice. Shut your eyes, let me finish.

Self-Portrait in Conflagration

An almost imperceptible shift in light,
a sudden low pressure, vertigo, a moment

of lessened gravity and tectonic
slippage. Then the Santa Anas with the sun

wildly filtering down. A hand reaches
from behind a tree and drops a match

that has not burned itself out; the palms
deadheaded by lightning; a mirror or cigarette,

accident or intended. In the center, a ring
of smoke and phosphorescence. Deer, graceless,

flee, tails bobbing unevenly, too long
and erotic. A wolf carrying something scavenged,

eyes sidelong, watches you. They know when to go;
can you say that for yourself in the kitchen?

You watch the approach. Squirming embers
that burn themselves out, then reignite

with each twig. The eucalyptus never smelled so sweet.
The linoleum, warm, grows hot. The kettle whistles,

a crack. How inferno feels from the inside:
a heavy sleep descending, gray then black.

From above, the house is a mirage.
Come closer, blink your eyes; it's gone.

Leavetaking

A river sixty miles down, curling through or surrounding
a city   *goodbye home   goodbye fields   goodbye cars*

your headlights on   sometimes an ocean, choppy blue or black
a red poppy in my lapel   goodbye wince   the white streaks

of motorboats, sailboats, coral reef.   *goodbye goodbye kiss
silent goodbye with lips moving*   Before the jolt of clouds,

some cool slices of pools   *goodbye nightmare   your hair
in my sheets*   scattered through yards, driveways. No matter

where you are   *goodbye the weather's turning and no coat
I'll just walk you out on*   the clouds,   *with a flock of geese overhead*

when you've passed through them, are the same, like a blinding
goodbye in a snow laden   field you'll never walk in.

There are no angels. You haven't called yet.   *goodbye I won't call*
Returning, the light on the tip of the wing looks like a plane

far off   *goodbye with averted eyes*   heading right towards you.
You can only stare; it's a long enough stare   *don't distract me*

to see what it is when the far off comes close. The air passing
your window   *hide the reminders*   makes the city lights flicker

like matches behind cupped hands.   *goodbye time zones
goodbye, meaning for now*   The sea is black and the sky above.

When you fall, it will be through a darker sky and the city lights
I don't know how   are the stars above us, brighter, closer.

Self-Portrait as Cannibal

I stuck my little dagger in you until the juices ran clear.
   Your chest, empty where your heart was. I pulled
it from its tethers, placed it in the freezer, cubed.

   Every night, I drop a piece in my pinot grigio;
      one is in there now, bleeding out a sweet cassis.
How does it feel to be an object, a collection really?

Every piece of you has its place. Your skin: cut in strips,
   braided into a rope that has many household purposes.
Your tongue: muffled in the garden. Ears: ashtrays.

   Your fingers: strung on a necklace, each nail
      screwed down with a precious stone. Bones:
wind chime. Your hair: a brooch, a symbol of my mourning.

Organs: sautéed. Muscles: smoked and cured to last me through
   winter. This house is a museum I've locked myself in.
I don't need anyone else, now that you are here to stay.

Notes

"Beckett Wolf": The majority of this poem is made up of lines taken from Samuel Beckett's short story "First Love" and Virginia Woolf's novel *Mrs. Dalloway*.

"Pastoral": The line, "I've come to understand all your lies // are like wishes" is based on the refrain from Wilco's song "Ashes of American Flags" from their album *Yankee Hotel Foxtrot*.

"Self-Portrait in Whirlwind": This poem takes lines from Johnny Cash's song "The Man Comes Around" from his record *American IV: The Man Comes Around*.

"The Spectators": The epigraph at the beginning is from Rainer Maria Rilke's "The Fifth Elegy" from *Duino Elegies*, translated by J.B. Leishman and Stephen Spender. Also, various lines have been taken from the first chapter of Richard Hughes' *A High Wind in Jamaica*.

"Looking at the Photographs": The majority of the italicized lines refer to photographs by Cecelia Post.

"How to Build the Island": The line, "Who chose this face for me?" is from *Ulysses* by James Joyce.

About the Author

Frances Justine Post is the recipient of the "Discovery"/*Boston Review* Poetry Prize, the Inprint Paul Verlaine Poetry Prize, and the Amy Award from *Poets & Writers*. Her poems have appeared in *American Letters & Commentary, Boston Review, Denver Quarterly, The Kenyon Review Online, The Massachusetts Review, Pleiades, Western Humanities Review,* and others. Originally from Sullivan's Island, SC, she received her MFA from Columbia University and is currently earning her PhD in Creative Writing at the University of Houston, where she is poetry editor for *Gulf Coast Magazine.*